PORTRAIT OF ALASKA

PORTRAIT OF
ALASKA

Photography by Nancy Simmerman, Fred Hirschmann, Kim Heacox, Tom Walker

Text by Hilary Hilscher

Graphic Arts Center Publishing®

International Standard Book Number 1-55868-356-9
Library of Congress Number 97-70472
Text, captions, and compilation of photographs © 1992, 1997
by Graphic Arts Center Publishing Company
P.O. Box 10306 • Portland, Oregon 97296-0306 • 503/226-2402
President • Charles M. Hopkins
Editor-in-Chief • Douglas A. Pfeiffer
Managing Editor • Jean Andrews
Production Manager • Richard L. Owsiany
Book Manufacturing • Lincoln & Allen Co.
Revised Edition
Printed in the United States of America

◄ ◄ Inside Passage. ▲ Grizzly or brown bear *(Ursus arctos)* in Denali
National Park and Preserve. ► Helicopters on Mendenhall Glacier.

Photo images: • pages 1, 2, 4, 5, 6, 10, 11, 12, 14, 15, 16, 17, 18, 19, 22, 23, 24-25, 27, 28, 29, 30, 31, 32, 33, 34, 35, 36-37, 38, 39, 41, 42, 43, 47, 48, 49, 51, 52-53, 60, 61, 63, 64, 65, 68-69, 73, 78, 79, back cover © 1992 by Nancy Simmerman • pages 8-9, 21, 26, 40, 44-45, 46, 50, 54, 56-57, 59, 72 © 1992; pages 58, 71, front cover © 1997 by Fred Hirschmann • pages 7, 55, 66, 67, 76, 77, 80 © 1992 by Tom Walker • page 62 © 1992; page 70 © 1997 by Kim Heacox • page 72 © 1992 by Mark Fraker/Courtesy of BP Exploration (Alaska) Inc. • page 75 © 1992 by Myron Wright/Courtesy of BP Exploration (Alaska) Inc.

◄ One of the world's great rivers, the twenty-three-hundred-mile Yukon flows—at times in channels up to twenty miles wide—from Canada through Alaska to the Bering Sea. ▲ Birds of prey, eagles grasp food in their talons while feeding or in flight. ► ► Thirty-five miles away, the 20,306-foot summit of Mount McKinley (Denali) looms above rolling hills near Thorofare Pass. Crystal clear skies occur on only a handful of summer days at Denali National Park and Preserve.

▲ A winter sun, reflected in the still waters of Auke Lake, kisses the Mendenhall Towers while Mendenhall Glacier slumbers in shadow. ▶ July's midnight sun blazes along the carrier of Alaska's "black gold." Completed in 1977, the pipeline stretches eight hundred miles from Prudhoe Bay across mountain ranges and rivers to tankers waiting at Valdez. Prudhoe crude oil supplies about one-seventh of America's daily requirement. ▶ ▶ Turnagain Arm's powerful incoming bore tide pushes seawater up the forty-mile-long Southcentral fjord.

ALASKAN LIGHT
by Hilary Hilscher

*When I returned to Alaska after sixteen years Outside,
the first thing that struck me was the quality of light. It
made me remember something deep inside I'd all but for-
gotten. It's hard to describe the feeling of Alaskan light on
a mountainside . . . but I get tears in my eyes when I see it.*

Alaskan Born in Fairbanks

I first discovered it when I was six: the world *Outside* is
different. For one thing, when I said *"Outside"* Outside, no
one knew what I meant. To Alaskans, *Outside,* spelled with a
capital O, means any place outside of Alaska, usually the
"Lower 48" or the contiguous United States. The expression
definitely captures the Alaskan frame of reference: Alaska—
the Great Land, the Last Frontier—forms the center of the
world . . . the rest is *Outside.*

Our attitude springs from the land itself: vast, long
uncharted, stunningly beautiful, natural, unpeopled, bounti-
ful and challenging. Even as we move more into the international mainstream via the economy, transportation, and
communication, Alaska—to Alaskans—remains our center.

But neither Alaskan terminology nor attitude accounted
for my awareness at age six. Nor was the world *Outside*
different merely because it took a long time to get there by
airplane. Like most Alaskan children, I'd grown up flying, so
taking a plane somewhere seemed normal.

Superimpose a map of Alaska onto one of the United
States, and this truly Great Land stretches from Florida to
California, from Texas to the Canadian border. Cut Alaska's
586,000 square miles in half, and Texas would become
the third-largest state. The tip of Southeast Alaska and our
westernmost point, Attu Island, lie over twenty-two hundred
miles apart. The international dateline bends far out around
the Aleutian Chain to include all of Alaska in today.

For some Alaskan kids, having a road that connects their
town with anywhere else would mark *Outside* as truly different. We still have several hundred communities unconnected
by highway. As one woman who grew up in Sitka on Baranof
Island put it, *"Outside,* you can drive for more than one hour
in one direction and not reach the end of the road! And you
can drive to other cities." Alaska's capital city, Juneau, can be
reached only by plane and boat. Glaciers and mountains have
so far thwarted road building to this mainland community.

At age six, I didn't realize that most places in America do
not have free-roaming wildlife the way Alaska does. Here are
moose (often right in town) plus brown, black and polar bear,
mountain sheep and goats, beaver and porcupine, caribou,
wolves and foxes, bald eagles, millions of shorebirds, and
marine life from whales and walrus to otters and seals.

So what makes it different *Outside?* The light. Or rather, the
lack of light. Here I was: *Outside* in the middle of summer and
it got *dark* at night! With all the certainty of a six-year-old, I
knew summertime means daylight. It gets dark in the *winter.*

The word Alaska comes from the Aleut *agunalaksh* or
Alyeska, meaning "Great Land." Alaska's size is just the
beginning of its "great" characteristics. Here are:

- 3,000,000 lakes larger than twenty acres;
- 3,000 rivers, including ten longer than 300 miles;
- 47,000 miles of shoreline, more than all the rest of the
  U.S. put together;
- 19 mountains higher than 14,000 feet, including North
  America's tallest peak, Mount McKinley or "Denali," at
  20,320 feet;
- 100,000 glaciers, more than half the world's total, with
  one larger than the state of Rhode Island.

Geologically, Alaska is young and restless, sitting pre-
cariously atop several colliding tectonic plates. Ten percent of
all the earthquakes on the planet occur here; North America's
strongest one hit Southcentral in 1964, measuring 9.2 on
today's Richter scale. Every year, one or more of our eighty
volcanoes erupts. Permafrost, permanently frozen ground,
lies under much of Alaska, and approximately 70 percent of
the state is treeless. Of all the states, we have the fewest
indigenous tree species (just thirty-three), and, as any Alaskan
or summer visitor will swear, we have the *most* mosquitoes.

For geography and climate, think of Alaska as five separate
states: Gulf of Alaska, the Interior, the Arctic, Bering Sea
Coast, and the Alaska Peninsula and Aleutians.

GULF OF ALASKA. This region begins with
Southeast, the six-hundred-mile-long "panhandle" snuggled
against Canada. Here is home to the country's largest national
forest, the Tongass, seventeen million acres of lush rainforest,
icefields and glaciers, rocky coast and inland waterways.

The Gulf's coastal region curves northwest then south, taking in Southcentral, the Kenai Peninsula, and the western side
of Cook Inlet. Like Southeast, this area features snowcapped
peaks plunging into gray-blue fjords, dense evergreen forest,
ice-free saltwater south of Anchorage, and heavy precipitation. Here is a spot wetter than any location in the Lower 48:
MacLeod Harbor on Montague Island gets more than 250
inches of rain a year. And Thompson Pass rates as one of the
snowiest places: more than eighty *feet* fell in winter 1952-53.
Inland areas are drier and cooler with sparser vegetation.

INTERIOR. The Alaska Range separates Southcentral
and the Gulf from the vast swath of Alaska's midsection: the
rolling hills, boreal forests, and great rivers of the Interior. The
state's greatest variety of temperatures occurs here. The record-
holders are Prospect Creek with -80° F, and Fort Yukon with
+100° F. Normal temperatures are only slightly less extreme.

ARCTIC. Marking the Interior's transition into the Arctic,
the Brooks Range rises treeless and jagged, then slopes gently
down, flattening into tundra plains. Ocean forms the northern boundary of this desert; less than five inches of precipitation falls annually at Point Barrow. It can snow all year round,
and ice masses remain in the offshore waters.

BERING COAST. This region of gentle hills, spacious
delta lands, and myriad river mouths around the western coast
of Alaska stretches from the Arctic to the Alaska Peninsula.

The Alaska Peninsula—together with Alaska's largest Island, Kodiak, the islands of the Bering Sea, and the thousand-mile-long Aleutian Chain—share a common maritime personality, rarely enjoying whole days of sunshine. Here the constants are fog, low clouds, heavy precipitation, high winds, high humidity. The average temperature varies just 25 degrees—from 30° F to 55° F throughout the year. Gale force winds gusting to more than seventy knots frequently blast the treeless, grassy islands of the Aleutians.

Outside, it's so much easier to be insulated from the light and the seasons and the weather. Here, people know they are not in charge: The weather is.

Fisherman in the Aleutians

Alaskans everywhere respond to the light. In our northernmost city, Barrow, summer's sun stays above the horizon for eighty-four days. In northern villages, people make their

Most non-perishables come from the Lower 48 by container ship or barge. This loaded vessel is in Womans Bay on Kodiak Island.

livelihoods with little regard for the clock: fishing, hunting, working, traveling. In large and small communities farther south, children and adults also respond to summer with a frenzied pace of work and recreation. Fairbanks folks mark summer solstice with the annual "Midnight Sun Baseball Game" which starts at 10:30 P.M. On clear nights, there's no need for stadium lights. Anchorage, which shares the 61° north latitude with Oslo, Helsinki, and St. Petersburg, Russia, finds people out on the bike trails during the nineteen hours of sun. Juneau residents take to the inland waterways of Southeast in their long hours of daylight.

Not only do the quantity of light and its cycles affect Alaskans in their everyday lives, the light's unique quality also produces a heaven on earth for photographers and artists. Because of the northern latitude, the sun never stands directly overhead. With its rays coming at an angle low to the horizon, they travel through more of the earth's atmosphere; the light is filtered into gentle tones. Always, long twilight

periods soften the edges of the day. Always, rich shadows stretch and linger. Summer sunsets are golden. Winter sunsets inundate snow-covered mountainsides with hours of alpenglow—luxurious pink and apricot cascading into royal velvet, dying into silver.

FIRST PEOPLES

Our ancestors were wise. They are still helping us today, singing to us through the masks. They are showing us to way to the future.

Yup'ik artist and writer

In the summer of 1989, a dozen Yup'ik Eskimo masks were returned to Western Alaska for examination by village elders. Museum curators from around the world didn't understand the masks and wanted to know their origins and purposes. As the elders talked, they began recalling images and stories from their childhoods, when shamans and spirits more directly dictated everyday Yup'ik life. The collective memory of the masks and accompanying songs and dances sparked a wave of historical interest among the Yup'ik.

In the past twenty-five years, indigenous cultures around the world have experienced a resurgence of pride in their own past. Alaskans, too, in an effort to preserve this traditional knowledge and wisdom, have been tape-recording elders' stories and writing down dying languages. Daily life skills are being remembered and taught to younger people. Songs are once again being sung, dances danced, and beliefs shared.

Sometimes I cannot remember how we expressed something. And now I cannot ask anyone anywhere anymore.

Last speaker of one Native language

In some cases, it's too late. A word, an entire language, or a village has gone extinct. What disease and massacre did not eliminate, missionaries and schooling and liquor nearly did. In the 250 years since European contact, Alaska's indigenous peoples have been enslaved, discriminated against, and forced to abandon their words and world views. Only within the past sixty years has the tide begun to change, as dominant white society revised laws and opinions. And only more recently still have Native peoples regained their voices, their lands, their pride. It is a struggle not yet ended, a tension yet to be resolved in Alaskan society as a whole.

The terms *Alaska Native* or *Native* with a capital *N* refer to the land's indigenous peoples, Eskimos, Indians, and Aleuts. Non-Native people born in Alaska are called native Alaskans. In the Bush, the roadless majority of Alaska, many villagers still rely, to varying degrees, on subsistence food-gathering from the land and waters. Native workers in the cities or oil fields often come home for the whale and caribou hunts. No longer dependent on spears, harpoons, or dogsleds, Native hunters rely on guns, motorboats, and snowmachines. They use CB radios to keep in touch with whaling crews in sealskin boats in the Arctic Ocean. Increasingly, however, the basic necessities of life come not from the land but from the store.

At the time of statehood in 1959, one dogteam still carried mail between two villages in the Arctic. Dog mushing survives today, but as sport only. Airlines and Bush planes now carry mail, people, and supplies to villages, camps, and homesteads throughout Alaska. In Southeast, the Alaska Marine Highway System, a state-run ferry boat service, connects formerly isolated communities with each other and Washington State. Communications in much of the Bush now mirror those available worldwide: faxes, computers hooked to the internet, phones, televisions, and VCRs.

Still, Bush Alaska encompasses a mix of tradition and the twenty-first century, of modern education and historical wisdom. It is a place where the old ways inspire, and where intimate knowledge of the land matters.

Alaska, the present-day "Last Frontier" was also America's "First Frontier." From 25,000 to 9,000 years ago, people migrated across the Bering Sea land "bridge," a broad, low-lying plain as much as a thousand miles wide, connecting Asia with North America. Current archeological thinking points to three main migrations. The first to come were the ancestors of most Indian peoples in South and North America. Second, the ancestors of the Navajo and Apache, the Athabaskans and the Tlingits. Finally, as recently as 4,000 years ago, the last ancestors of today's Eskimos and Aleuts arrived. As the glaciers of the last ice age melted, the sea rose, covering the bridge and separating the two continents. Today, Alaska and the Russian Far East lie fifty-six miles apart across the Bering Strait.

Four main ethnic groups established homeland boundaries, each adapting to the particular geography, weather, and food supply of its region. In spite of the harsh climate, the north country provided sustenance adequate for human beings to not only survive, but to evolve and prosper. Alaska's first peoples developed rich mythologies, arts, and customs; they traveled and traded and waged war. Their traditions included reverence for the spirit world, inextricably interwoven with people and all natural elements. Their unique knowledge and skills enabled these communal societies to sustain themselves over thousands of years.

Historically, the Athabaskan Indians roamed the great Interior, leading a spartan, semi-nomadic life to follow game along the rivers and tributaries, through the boreal forests and across muskeg flats. Living in small bands, these exceptional survivalists traveled on foot year-round, supplemented by birchbark canoes on water during summer. Always, they faced severe temperature extremes and an uncertain food supply. Comprised of many regional groups, the Athabaskans extended their territory south into the Copper River and Cook Inlet areas of Southcentral.

The Athabaskans' sometime trading partners, distrusted neighbors, and opponents in battle were the Eskimos. While some Eskimo groups migrated inland with the caribou, the saltwater coast sculpted their civilizations—the Inupiat in the Arctic, the Yup'ik in Western Alaska, and smaller groups in the eastern Aleutians, Kodiak, and Prince William Sound. Individually, they hunted marine mammals in skin kayaks, but the truly astounding hunt was communal. Whaling involved the whole village in its practice and rituals. Men in large open skin boats harpooned the whale, then everyone helped haul it in and divided the catch among all households.

In Alaska's more temperate areas the Aleut people dwelled in the West; the Tlingit, Haida, and Tsimsian in Southeast. In a sweeping arc of twelve hundred miles, the grassy, volcanic peaks of the Aleutian Islands form a porous divide between the icy Bering Sea and the restless North Pacific Ocean. The Aleut people lived partially underground in earthen lodges, and crafted distinctive bentwood hats, intricate woven baskets, and waterproof clothing. They harvested an ample livelihood from shore and sea. The Aleuts plied the world's worst waters in tiny skin kayaks, water-proofing their craft by attaching their gut parkas tightly over the opening in which they sat—the same method used by kayakers today.

Sled dogs are bred for sprints—short races up to thirty miles— and for marathons like the Kuskokwim 300 and the Iditarod.

In Alaska's Southeast lived the peoples of the rainforest, misty fjords, and inland waterways. The arts flourished in many forms, including epic storytelling, carving, and weaving. The Haida crafted long, seagoing canoes from single trees while the Tlingits excelled at fashioning totem poles and elaborate clan housefronts. Patterned blankets, hats, and dance objects were created by all three groups for everyday use and as gifts during potlatches. Elaborate kinship patterns dictated authority and etiquette; wars and slavery were commonplace.

Though historically Alaska's Native peoples often fought with each other, and lived quite distinct lifestyles in separate regions of the state, they shared one deep, abiding value: their connection with the land. This shared value led them to unite in the mid-twentieth century against infringement on their way of life that had begun in the 1740s. That's when the Russians discovered Alaska's wealth of fur. So began the rush for Alaska's riches, which marked the end of Native isolation from the Western world.

During the long years they occupied Russian America, the Russians made no treaties or other land-ownership arrangements with Alaska's aboriginal people. When the United States purchased Alaska in 1867, the Americans simply guaranteed the Native peoples their "historical rights," without bothering to define what that meant.

The Alaska Statehood Act of 1959 entitled the state to select about 103 million acres from Alaska's federal holdings, which comprised nearly all the land. By giving the new state title to land containing potentially valuable resources, Congress hoped the fledgling government would become economically self-sufficient. But when the state began to choose its acreage and publicize its ambitious plans for resource development, it ran into the Native people. Alaska's Natives filed claims to land by right of original occupancy and use. The Secretary of the Interior appointed a mostly Native committee to draft legislation, and the issue moved into the halls of Congress. In 1968, Alaska's Native people gained an unexpected and unlikely ally: the oil industry.

One in forty-five Alaskans holds a pilot's license. Near Anchorage at Lakes Hood and Spenard lies the world's largest floatplane base.

North America's largest oil field had been discovered on Alaska's North Slope. A pipeline to carry the oil to market could not be built until title to lands along the route was settled. Oil companies joined the state government and Alaska's Congressional delegation in a final push. In December 1971, the Alaska Native Claims Settlement Act was passed. The legislation awarded the state's Native people nearly one billion dollars in cash and forty-four million acres of land.

This settlement, unlike others with Native Americans in the Lower 48, gave administrative power to the Native people themselves. Rather than direct the payments to individuals, Congress chose to structure the distribution through corporations, an effort to bring Native people more into the Western economy, and to avoid problems experienced by reservations Outside. Native corporations differ from most public corporations in that their directors are also owners, stockholders, and generally related to each other and the stockholders. Native corporations are legally mandated to strive for profits.

But since education, employment, social, and housing needs are also great, non-profit Native corporations have been established to address these issues. Ironically, the very Act which gave Alaska's Eskimo, Indian, and Aleut people legal title to their historic lands has also propelled them into the economic fast lane of Western society. Some corporations are hugely profitable; some are in difficulty.

In one way, the Act succeeded spectacularly: it helped unite Native people throughout the state around common concerns: legal, social, economic, political, and cultural. And it has made the immigrants to this Great Land—people not of Native ancestry—more aware of the connection between the land and all its peoples.

Which brings us back to the Yup'ik masks. The return of the masks to Western Alaska and the resurgence of interest in ancestral practices grew into a remarkable museum exhibit of more than fifty masks. Appropriately, the exhibit opened first in Western Alaska, then moved on to Anchorage, to New York, and to Washington, D.C. The masks reveal a world where spirits and people lived in close communication, aided by powerful shamans. The masks harken back to communal dancing and singing, of welcoming the spring, and honoring the animals on whom the people depended. Not only is this exhibit inherently exciting, it also symbolizes the long road Alaska's Native peoples have traveled to arrive at a position of respect in Western society.

TALES OF RICHES

The Russians were drawn by Alaska's "soft gold," the furs. They wrote the first chapter in this state's continuing history of natural resource-based rushes: the influx of *Outsiders* to utilize the wealth of land and sea. By the end of the 1700s, freebooting hunters had nearly exterminated fur seals and sea otters in the Aleutians. The Russians moved east: to Kodiak, Southcentral, then Southeast to maintain their fur trade.

Intrigued by exploration and the riches of this land, Europeans—the Spanish, English, and French—and later the Americans appeared on the scene. They charted coast and rivers, renamed local geographic features, and traded with Native peoples. The Russian America Company maintained its Alaskan empire against incursions by other nations well into the 1800s. The company ruled from its headquarters in Sitka. This capital city was known among seafarers as the "Paris of the Pacific" for its many comforts of European high society.

Faced by declining fur harvests and the need for cash at home, an emissary of the Czar approached the United States with a real estate deal. Spurred on by the belief that America's "manifest destiny" lay in stretching from coast to coast, the U.S. agreed to buy Alaska for less than two cents an acre. In the wee hours of the morning on March 30, 1867, Secretary of State William H. Seward handed over to the Russian ambassador a check for $7,200,000.

The American press and Congress were less than enthusiastic. "Seward's Folly!" they lamented, and dubbed this vast territory, "Walrussia," and "Seward's Icebox." Because so little was known about the land, government and private interests sponsored a number of scientific and exploratory expeditions to Alaska. The powers in Washington, D.C., however, had little interest in actually taking charge of their far-flung territory. They virtually ignored it for the next thirty years.

Then came gold. Gold-seekers began trickling into the north country in the 1840s and found the yellow metal in the Fortymile country in the Interior and inland from Cook Inlet in Southcentral. They struck rich veins in Southeast in the 1880s, and founded the city of Juneau. Then, in July of 1897, the steamer *Portland* docked in Seattle with its triumphant miners and precious cargo. "TON OF GOLD" screamed the headlines. The rush was on.

I grew up on stories of the Gold Rush. My father loved recounting the tales of his father in the Klondike. How Grandfather made a dozen trips over Chilkoot Pass, the most-used route to the gold fields in Canada. Daddy described how Grandfather brought in sheep, cattle, and pigs to provide food for the miners. And how he always did a little prospecting on the side, hoping to leave his butcher's trade behind for golden riches. How he traveled to Alaska for seventeen years, hooked on the adventure and the challenge. How once, in 1907, my grandmother, my toddler father, and his brother came north, too, riding in comfort to the gold country on the new White Pass and Yukon Railroad. In Whitehorse, the family boarded a barge loaded with sheep and cattle bound for Fort Yukon in Alaska's Interior. They planned to spend a winter there, their first winter together in ten years. They never made it.

On the Yukon River's notorious Five-Finger Rapids, the barge swamped and started to break apart. The livestock spilled into the water. Men on the shore saw the disaster unfolding, and rushed in boats to pluck the family off the disintegrating barge. Back on shore, my grandmother, quite soggy and frightened, pulled herself up to her full five feet three inches and shook her finger at my very tall grandfather. "This country just isn't civilized yet!" she declared, and took her two young sons back to Seattle.

My father was 76 years old when he and I retraced his father's path into the Klondike over the Chilkoot Trail, which has become an international historic park. As we hiked, those tales of '98 sprung to life. We stepped in Grandfather's foot-falls along the Taiya River. We climbed the "Golden Stairs," the last sheer rockfall before the border that still requires hand-over-hand scrambling. And we cheered at the first sight of azure Lake Bennett at the end of the modern route.

We paused often along the trail to wonder at the belongings discarded by those early gold-seekers: rusted tools, worn shoes, rotting knapsacks. (Of course, we wondered whether any had once been our family's possessions.) Now, everything along the way is protected—moot testimony to the twenty to thirty thousand gold seekers who passed this way. The early Alaska tales my father told live on still in a wood-and-tin steamer trunk in my storage closet, chock-full of diaries and other mementos of Grandfather's Gold Rush.

The floodtide of miners into the Klondike in '98 washed on into Alaska. After 1900, prospectors struck gold at nearly thirty locations from Nome to Southcentral. With government nearly non-existent in the north country, "miners' justice" frequently prevailed. Reports decried an Alaska without law and order or schools. The United States finally responded. Initially, Congress passed a criminal code and other provisions, then approved full territorial status in 1912. Seven years before the U.S. adopted the Nineteenth Amendment, the first act of Alaska's new legislature was to give women the vote.

In the early 1900s, J. P. Morgan and the Guggenheim Brothers developed the rich Kennecott Copper Mine in the Wrangell Mountains. Ore was moved by rail almost two hundred miles to Cordova.

In the 1900s, salmon fishing largely replaced whaling, which had dominated the harvest in the 1800s. From Western Alaska to the Inside Passage, *Outside* owners paid for million-dollar canneries in a single season, enjoying the relative freedom from government constraint in the territory.

The state flower, the forget-me-not, decorates alpine meadows and streambeds from Southeast to the Arctic to the Aleutians.

In 1914, construction began on the Alaska Railroad, headquartered at a tiny settlement on Cook Inlet in Southcentral. They named the community, Anchorage. Huge implications for the future occurred eight years later, with the 1922 landing in Ketchikan of Alaska's first commercial airplane. At last, here was transportation equal to the challenge of Alaska's vast landscape, mile-wide rivers, and towering mountain ramparts.

In 1935, Alaska made headlines across the country as the site of a bold agricultural and social experiment. More than two hundred farm families from the Dust Bowl of the Midwest relocated with federal assistance to Southcentral Alaska's Matanuska Valley. While Alaska's agricultural sector has never realized its much-hoped-for potential, some farming still persists. The ninety-pound cabbages at the State Fair each fall form an impressive legacy of these early agricultural "colonists."

If strategic location can be considered a natural resource, this Alaska resource received high priority for development when World War II broke out. The United States military invested nearly a billion dollars in Alaska during the war. In less than nine months, troops punched through the Alaska-Canada (or Alcan) route, now known as the Alaska Highway. Alaska was finally connected to the rest of the country by road. Troops built other roads, airfields, and installations, and fought off a Japanese invasion of the Aleutian Islands, the only North American soil occupied by Axis powers.

Alaska's population ballooned from 74,000 in 1941 to more than 120,000 by the end of the war. Drillers found oil on the Kenai Peninsula, commercial fishing prospered, and the U.S. Forest Service began opening land to logging. Alaskans wanted more local control; they wanted statehood. Just as the country had been reluctant to fully accept its new purchase a century before, the United States government was slow to make Alaska a full-fledged partner in the Union. The canned salmon industry, especially, was happy with the status quo, and wanted no additional regulations or restrictions. Intense lobbying, the drafting of a model constitution, and

The University of Alaska-Anchorage Library serves its own students as well as those who attend Alaska Pacific University.

the election of unofficial delegates to Congress finally turned the tide. With high hopes, Alaskans began their modern era as residents of the Forty-ninth State on January 3, 1959.

From statehood on, Alaska's development can be explained almost entirely in one word: oil. The first oil lease sales by the new government came during its first year, and wells began producing on the Kenai Peninsula. Nine years later eight thousand feet under Alaska's North Slope, Atlantic Richfield discovered a "supergiant" oil field at Prudhoe Bay.

THE POWER OF OIL

Alaska's Arctic had oil. But how to get it to market? A consortium of eight oil companies formed to build the largest private construction project in history. The task? To design an eight-hundred-mile pipeline to carry crude oil safely over Arctic tundra and permafrost, three mountain ranges, major earthquake fault zones, more than 350 rivers and

streams, to tanks and tankers at the ice-free port of Valdez in Southcentral. At a cost of $8 billion, the pipeline became history's most expensive project to date, and from an environmental standpoint, the most closely scrutinized one.

In 1974, construction began by building a road north—spanning the Yukon River and on to the Arctic Ocean. Less than a year later, I followed my grandfather's example. I quit my professional job and signed up at a union hall. Hardhat in hand, I became one of the twenty-two thousand people making exorbitant wages working on the pipeline. This was my "gold rush."

We pipeliners formed a fluid workforce. Our number at any one time varied by several thousand depending on the season and construction timetable. By the end of the three-year project, the pipeline had employed more than seventy thousand people: young and mature, seasoned and green, educated and unschooled, Americans and foreigners, dedicated workers and dilettantes. Women and Natives received their first real taste of construction work. It was a heady time of adventure and accomplishment.

"Oil-in" came June 20, 1977, providing up to one-fifth of the U.S. demand for crude oil. Since the Prudhoe Bay field underlies Alaska-owned land, the industry pays a royalty to the state for extracting the resource. The influx of petro dollars fueled state spending on a multitude of things Alaskans lacked—or wanted! Appropriations from state coffers funded facilities like Bush schools and urban civic centers, libraries, and art centers; and social programs like cash bonuses to senior citizens and repeal of property taxes.

Before the oil began flowing, a far-sighted governor, aided by the legislature, set up a trust fund for the people of Alaska. The Alaska Permanent Fund, now the largest trust in the country, distributes dividends to all Alaskans in the form of annual checks up to $1,000. The principal is protected and inflation-proofed every year—and is growing.

While Prudhoe Bay was gigantic, the oil industry knew production would begin to decline in the 1990s. Companies continued exploring and producing fields on and offshore in the Arctic. They especially wanted access to the adjacent nineteen-million-acre Arctic National Wildlife Refuge, the calving ground of the Porcupine caribou herd. Supported by many Alaskans, a lobbying effort began in Washington, D.C.

Scientific research on the "Slope" and along the pipeline route, funded largely by industry, has been extensive. Studies are providing much valuable information about the land, waters, and wildlife of the region. Companies are proud of their environmental records. However, some Native people and other Alaskans, and some people who live in other places have concerns about the long-term compatibility of major industry and natural ecosystems—concern that reached a crescendo on Good Friday, March 24, 1989.

The supertanker Exxon Valdez sent a transmission to the Coast Guard saying it was "fetched up hard aground on Bligh Reef," the best-known hazard in Prince William Sound. The tanker's full load of Alaskan crude was spewing into biologically rich waters, a spill that would grow to nearly eleven million gallons and spread over six hundred square miles through the Sound and across the Gulf to the Alaskan Peninsula. The noxious goo and froth affected fish, marine mammals, birds, people, and parklands. By 1997, research showed that one of the species harmed by the spill, the bald eagle, had fully recovered. Others are holding their own or are still in decline. Exxon was forced to pay $900 million and the cost of cleanup and restoration of the Alaskan coastline.

Research three years after the spill showed that about 70 percent of the oil had biodegraded or evaporated, about 14 percent had been recovered, and the rest remained in the water and soil. Today, the Sound appears pristine once again; visitors can see wildlife. But people who knew the Sound, people who relied on its bounty for their food, say it's not the same. Perhaps time will heal the wildlife and land and communities. Meanwhile, many steps have been taken by Alaska's companies, citizens, and governments to guard against another such disaster.

As of 1997, the Arctic National Wildlife Refuge remains closed to drilling. With oil prices high and new technology, oil companies are now producing formerly unprofitable fields and looking to the National Petroleum Reserve-Alaska as a new frontier. The state government views itself more as a partner with industry; after all, oil pays 85 percent of the government's bills. Yes, oil wrought big changes in Alaska, changes with both sweet benefits and dear costs. Yet for all this, our vistas still mostly match Robert Service's description:

It's the great big broad land 'way up yonder,
It's the forest where silence has lease;
It's the beauty that thrills me with wonder,
It's the stillness that fills me with peace.

NATURAL BOUNTY

Barely beyond the edges of our communities lies the Alaska of myth and wonder. Within easy reach everywhere lie parklands. State parklands and national parklands, publicly owned forests and refuges, wilderness preserves, monuments, recreation areas, historic sites, wildlife sanctuaries, and wild and scenic rivers—more than 161 million acres in all, more than 44 percent of Alaska. These protected areas promise that our children and their children will know Alaska's natural heritage as intimately as we have been privileged to know it.

From the sky-piercing rock fingers of the Arrigetch Peaks in Gates of the Arctic National Park to the vast floodplain of Yukon Flats National Wildlife Refuge; from hot summer days in the desert of Kobuk Valley National Park to frigid Aurora-filled nights in Tetlin National Wildlife Refuge; from the largest sanctuary for brown bears on the Alaska Peninsula to the world's greatest nesting population of bald eagles on Admiralty Island—here are treasures for all Americans.

The Alaska Maritime National Wildlife Refuge stretches from the tip of Southeast to the state's northwest corner: a salt-sprayed potpourri of some twenty-four hundred islands, reefs, headlands, rocks, and spires. This refuge protects the largest marine bird population in the Northern Hemisphere: it is home to more than twenty million seabirds, about two-thirds of Alaska's summer total. Misty Fiords National Monument in Southeast encompasses cloud-shrouded cliffs that rise higher than those in Yosemite Valley. It has blue-green waterways, dense forests, cascading waterfalls, wild rivers, and clear alpine lakes.

One of the world's largest volcanic craters forms the six-mile-wide centerpiece of remote and restless Aniakchak National Monument, Preserve and Wild River. Nearby, Katmai National Park and Preserve embraces a desolate moonscape left by the 1912 ash flow that buried a twenty-mile-long valley in pumice and ash. In Northwestern Alaska, nearly the entire watershed of the Noatak River, which accommodates 350-mile-long float trips, is classified as wilderness.

On the opposite side of the state, more than three-fourths of the 13.3-million-acre Wrangell-Saint Elias National Park and

At the Arctic Slope Regional Corporation and Stuaqpak Store, Inupiat Natives take advantage of the local bus service in Barrow.

Preserve is now designated wilderness. This rugged retreat contains North America's greatest collection of glaciers, including the Bagley Icefield, which measures 190 miles long and 4,000 feet thick; and the Malaspina Glacier, which is half again the size of Delaware. Within park borders soar the continent's greatest concentration of peaks over 16,000 feet, including Mount Saint Elias, second-highest peak in the U.S. at 18,008 feet. This largest of all U.S. parks adjoins Canada's spectacular Kluane National Park and Tatshinshini Wilderness forming the largest protected landscape on the planet.

The 114 beach sand ridges of Cape Krusenstern National Monument contain artifacts of every known Eskimo occupation of North America since 6000 B.C., while the Bering Land Bridge National Preserve was established to protect resources used by local Native people in their subsistence lifestyle. Other parklands preserve areas of Alaska's history: Castle Hill and Old Sitka State Parks, historic sites commemorating the Russian Period. Totem Bight State Historic Park features nineteenth-century totem poles carved by Tlingit and Haida Indians. Iditarod National Historical Trail and Independence Mine State Historic Park recall Alaska's gold mining past; and Fort Abercrombie State Historic Park memorializes World War II.

No list of Alaska's parklands would be complete without mention of four that see the most human visitors: Chugach National Forest's Portage Glacier, Glacier Bay, Chugach State Park, and Denali. The most visited spot in Alaska beckons just fifty miles from Anchorage, Alaska's largest city. A paved highway leads to the shore of a milky lake filled with blue meringue icebergs, calved from Portage Glacier at the lake's far end. Now in retreat, the glacier's face can be reached by tour boat. The glacier gained its name from its historic usefulness to Tanaina Indians, Chugach Eskimos and European traders, who "portaged" across it between Prince William Sound and Cook Inlet.

Though Anchorage's human population is near 230,000, a hearty wildlife population inhabits our very backyard. Federal, state, and local parks comprise much of the municipality of Anchorage. Most familiar to residents is the five-hundred-thousand-acre Chugach State Park, its edges laced with trails and camping spots. Thriving in the natural world of the Park backcountry are wolves, brown bears, lynx, ermine, mink, foxes, plus many smaller furry and feathered creatures.

In the 1790s, Captain George Vancouver sailed through Southeast mapping and recording geographic features. He scarcely noticed a slight indentation in an icefield several miles thick that filled a bay nearly to its headlands. Now, two centuries later, the glaciers have retreated, exposing numerous inlets in a bay sixty-five miles long. Sixteen sapphire tidewater glaciers plunge into blue-green, ice-choked fjords rimmed by tide-scoured beaches—designated as Glacier Bay National Park and Preserve.

In reverence and awe, the Athabaskans called it Denali, "the high one." Most Alaskans still feel the same way. And we, too, call it Denali. This name also refers to the immense Interior conservation area that straddles the broad midsection of the Alaska Range. This section contains Denali and Menlale, "Denali's Wife": Mt. Foraker, at 17,395 feet. From the perpetually snow-covered massif, the land sweeps down into broad valleys with braided rivers, rolling spruce forests, and tundra steppes dotted with kettle ponds and creeks. Called the "greatest subarctic sanctuary" on earth, bear, moose, caribou, and wolves roam Denali Park freely.

Denali National Park, like Alaska's other accessible parklands and other parklands around the world, faces a specter. This is the ironic risk of being "loved to death." On one hand, Alaska stands to gain staunch allies as people come to experience our wild lands. On the other hand, it's a challenge to strike the right balance between human access—and the need of wildlife and landscape to be left alone. As the human population on earth increases, so will pressure on remaining wild places. In the end, Alaska's truest gift may be what we leave alone rather than what we "develop."

SHARING DREAMS

Always the land reminds us: we are its guests. It shapes us. We people, together with the land, create who we are and what we dream.

Alaskan homesteader

Alaska society is beginning to reflect the wide world *Outside*. We come from many ethnic backgrounds. We represent different lengths of residency, and have varying ideas of how long we'll stay. We want a sense of community, whether in the Bush or city. And we're faced with constant change.

It's easy to make judgments about new versus old, to want things to stay the same. But as one neighbor puts it, "Once you encounter something new, you change too. What matters is what you keep as values and how you live them."

With just over half a million people, Alaska is among the states with the fewest number of residents. If Manhattan Island's population density matched ours, fewer than twenty people would live there! Yet, since the mid-1970s, Alaska has been growing at one of the country's fastest rates. In the 1980s alone, the state's population soared nearly 40 percent.

Alaska's smaller population also means everyone has the opportunity to do more, from participating in civic organizations to serving on boards and commissions. And we are avid networkers. Newcomers and visitors quickly realize it's difficult to say something in one community without its preceding them to the next. "Everybody here knows everyone else—from Ketchikan to Barrow!" a national news producer once declared in astonishment.

I don't think Alaskans are truly different from other people. I just think our free and plentiful opportunities allow us to come maybe a little closer to our God-given potential.

Alaskan Broadcasting Pioneer

Many Alaskans shake our heads in amazement at today's headlong pace of change. While we relish economic vigor, we also worry that Alaska may be losing its "specialness."

People who have just moved north and people who visit see Alaska through fresher eyes. They see what is here rather than what has changed. To these cheechakoes, these newcomers, we ask, "Why did you come? What have you found?"

They describe grandeur and magic. They talk about energy, freedom, opportunity. They remark on the cycles of the midnight sun and darkness. They marvel at the dancing hues of the Northern Lights. They thrill to the vibrant sunrise and become pensive in the quiet sunset. They talk about the unusual sunshine that imparts a rich quality to the land.

We know that light. That vitality and magnetism. That peace. The Alaska they describe is the same Alaska that has drawn people throughout history. We have come to adventure, to contribute, and to be at home. We hear the words that describe the Alaska we know—and we are reassured.

◄ ◄ Dark stripes of rubble—medial moraines—meander down the Russell Glacier. Snow feeding the glacier falls on University Range, of which Mounts Churchill and Bona are visible. ▲ Juneau International Airport sprawls over the valley carved by the mile-wide Mendenhall Glacier. Southeast residents rely heavily on air service—float planes, wheeled Bush aircraft, and commercial jets. ► Crafty Raven releases the sun into the firmament while the Old Man, his grandfather, looks on, in Naa Kahidi Theater's dramatization of a Tlingit creation myth.

◄◄ Riggs is one of the sixteen active, tidewater glaciers that converge in the crystalline splendor of Glacier Bay National Park and Preserve. ◄ The Juneau Icefield dwarfs a Wings of Alaska Cessna 206. ▲ The MV *Columbia,* a 418-foot ship of the Marine Highway System, and its sister ships provide regularly scheduled service between numerous Southeastern ports and the Lower 48 via Bellingham. Locals laughingly call them "Blue Canoes." Another section of the marine system links ports in Southwestern Alaska.

▲ Glacier Bay barely appears on explorer George Vancouver's charts, because in 1794 it was only a slight indentation in an immense river of ice. Since then, retreating ice has left a fjord sixty-five miles long. ▶ Lovely, violet lupine—a "colonizing" plant that enriches the soil after glacial retreat—grows to four feet in height during the nearly twenty-four-hour daylight of summer.

◄ Stalks of Indian paintbrush brighten a salt chuck on a characteristically misty day. ▲ Tlingit Indian carver Nathan Jackson applies accent paint to a cedar totem at Saxman Totem Park outside of Ketchikan, one of several cultural centers where visitors can watch artists producing traditional Southeast Native crafts.

▲ "Flightseeing" by small plane or helicopter provides a thrilling look at such spectacular scenes as Big Goat Lake in Misty Fiords National Monument. ▶ A helicopter hovers between a waterfall and a rainbow in the Ferebee River valley near Skagway.

◄ From October through January, a chum salmon run draws three thousand bald eagles—the world's largest known congregation—to a section of the Chilkat River known locally as the Chilkat Bald Eagle Council Grounds. ▲ A reminder of Old World heritage, Norwegian tole painting decorates Petersburg homes and businesses. Residents celebrate the "Little Norway Festival" in May with dancing, costumes, Viking ships, and Scandinavian food. ► ► Mount Edgecumbe, an extinct volcano visible from Sitka, rises Fuji-like from Kruzof Island.

▲ Weathered cannery buildings and derelict fishing boats provide picturesque sketch material for artists in Haines (population 1,800). Situated at the northern end of the salmon-rich Lynn Canal, Haines supports a sizable gill net fleet. ▶ The seine-caught salmon will be iced and stored in the hold until they can be off-loaded to a cannery tender or dock for processing.

◄ Situated in Sitka, the altar in the Chapel of the Annunciation in the Russian Bishop's House has been restored to its 1853 appearance. Russian Orthodox services are still held here occasionally.
▲ A brown bear sow and cub move with amazing ease along the sheer cliffs of this glacial fjord. Known also as grizzlies, brown bears inhabit the mainland and islands of Southeast and Southcentral Alaska; a favorite food is spawning salmon.

▲ Two residents of Kodiak, home to thirteen thousand people, stroll along Ugak Bay, part of the mountainous island's eight-hundred-mile coastline. ▶ One of five frozen cascades spilling down from the Kenai Mountains south of Kachemak Bay, Dixon Glacier presents an icy contrast to the rich autumn pastureland of a Homer farm. ▶ ▶ Almost eighty years after the cataclysmic eruption of Novarupta, fireweed reappears in the Valley of Ten Thousand Smokes.

◄ When red salmon run in mid-July, brown bears stake out prime fishing spots at Brooks Falls. ▲ In the 1930s, federally relocated farmers fleeing the Midwest's Dust Bowl colonized Southcentral's Matanuska Valley north of Anchorage. The short growing season's long daylight hours produce eighty-pound cabbages and other gigantic vegetables, which are spotlighted each fall at the Alaska State Fair.

▲ In the soft September light, cottonwoods display their burnished gold leaves against the primeval milieu of Kachemak Bay's Grewingk Glacier. ▶ On the Alaska Peninsula, Hallo Creek illustrates the land-sculpting technique of the state's numerous glacial rivers. Sediment deposited by the water continually fills in streambeds, forcing the water to create new channels and to braid itself around gravel bars.

◄ Southeast of Chitistone River, the rugged peaks of the University Range are capped with glacial ice. ▲ Alaska's strategic location received international attention during World War II; the military rapidly constructed roads, airfields, and installations in the territory. Today, along with adjacent Fort Richardson, Elmendorf Air Force Base forms an important part of America's northern line of defense. During Armed Forces Day Open House, the public from nearby Anchorage inspects the latest military aircraft and equipment.

◄ ◄ Columbia Glacier flows forty-one miles out of the Chugach
Mountains and releases icebergs which drift in the ocean currents of
the scenic Prince William Sound, frequented by pleasure craft and
oil tankers. ▲ With parallel airstrips plus Hardenburg Bay, wheel and
float planes are provided access to the village of Port Alsworth on
Lake Clark. With a population of only fifty permanent residents, a
busy summer afternoon can still find bush planes stacked up waiting
to land. ► A strip of velvet persists on a bull moose's antlers.

◄ ◄ Bush planes return to the Lake Hood Airstrip as a full moon rises above Anchorage. ◄ Balsam poplars and white spruce frame a peak of the Chugach Range beyond Thunderbird Creek in Alaska's Chugach State Park. ▲ An autumn scene of Goat Mountain and Twin Peaks of the Chugach Range are reflected in the serene waters of Cottonwood Lake in the Matanuska Valley, Alaska.

▲ On shedding August velvet, the male caribou's antlers glow with the color of exposed blood vessels for a few hours until their surface hardens and darkens. Unlike other members of the deer family, both male and female caribou *(Rangifer tarandus)* grow antlers. ▶ George Parks Highway, linking Anchorage and Fairbanks, crosses the Alaska Range over Broad Pass. At twenty-three hundred feet, this pass is one of the lowest divides in North America. On its north side, rivers drain into the Yukon; rivers on the south side flow into Cook Inlet.

◄ A musher glides beneath a bluff at sunset on the Yukon River, between Ruby and Galena on the Iditarod Trail Sled Dog Race.
▲ A private residence in Fairbanks, Alaska's second largest city, which lies in the vast Tanana River Valley. Begun after a gold discovery in 1903, the community boomed as the supply source for nearby mining activity. Today, it remains a supply and service center for Interior and Arctic industrial activities.

▲ Beckoning through the darkness of a winter afternoon, lights illuminate a log cabin at Alaskaland, Fairbanks' pioneer park of historic buildings and shops, dance halls and theaters, restaurants and playgrounds. ▶ Centuries of irresistable pressure by advancing walls of ice created the Great Gorge of the Ruth Glacier. More than twenty glaciers which flow from the Mount McKinley (Denali) massif measure five to forty miles in length.

◄ Dall sheep *(Ovis dalli dalli)* are born in May or June in mountain retreats. In summer, while the ewes travel downhill to feed, lambs gather in playful nursery groups, which are often supervised by a single ewe. ▲ Although the cock has a showy red eye comb, the female spruce grouse *(Canachites canadensis)* blends perfectly with her environment. In autumn, grouse seek grit to process their winter food of spruce needles. ►► Climbers carry gear to an air taxi on the snowy runway of Kahiltna Glacier's "international airport." Mount McKinley's south face looms in the center background.

◄ Champion musher Jeff King drives a team of huskies down the snowy road that leads to his home near Denali National Park, Alaska. ▲ Morning light reflects the Arrigetch Peaks off Arrigetch Creek. Most of the Brooks Range is composed of sedimentary rock. However, at the Arrigetch, the granitic core of the range is exposed. Glacial carving and the slightly curving exfoliation peculiar to granite has sculpted cliffs, domes, and knife ridges.

▲ North Slope Borough Search and Rescue's Bell 214 Super Transport delivers emergency radio equipment to the vessel, Big Valley, trapped by pack ice northwest of Barrow. ▶ Inupiat Eskimos at Wainwright haul in a bowhead whale using blocks left by whaling ships; in Wainright, as in most Inupiat Eskimo communities, whaling is a traditional activity involving the whole village.

◄ The sculpted surface of the snow is evidence of the persistent wind, while North Slope oil field facilities operate in the semi-darkness of a winter day. In December and January when the sun does not rise, a silvery twilight bathes the landscape in pale light for several hours a day. ▲ The steeply angled strata of Slope Mountain at the northern fringe of the Brooks Range provide a dramatic backdrop for the Trans-Alaska Pipeline as it heads south for Valdez. Numerous marine fossils indicate that the area was once submerged under an ancient sea.

▲ Puffin eggs have been used as food by humans for centuries. In order to fly, the bird must dive from cliffs, or when on water, "run" to become airborne. ▶ Preyed on by killer whales and polar bears, walrus are also hunted by Alaska Natives and Russians, who prize both the meat and the ivory.

◄ Scientists believe the eerie Aurora Borealis results from charged
solar particles which, on striking the earth's atmosphere, create the
spectacular colored lights. Ancient Native legends say the undulating
Northern Lights come from torches lighting the way to heaven for
departed souls. ▲ Though little snow falls overall in the arid Arctic,
the howling winter winds pack drifts up to the rooftops. These
Kotzebue children scrambled up nature's walkway to one of the
highest spots in town—a perfect place to frolic.

▲ *Ursus maritimus,* the polar bear, is a powerful hunter of seals. Male polar bears grow up to ten feet long. Females are smaller. Study of the bears is made difficult by their seasonal movements and by changes in the distribution of the Arctic ice. However, one radio-tracking experiment indicated they were usually found to den on the ice pack.